T0162363

ISLE OF THE SIGNATORIES

ISLE OF THE SIGNATORIES

POEMS

MARJORIE WELISH

COFFEE HOUSE PRESS

MINNEAPOLIS

2008

COPYRIGHT © 2008 by Marjorie Welish
COVER ART by Marjorie Welish
AUTHOR PHOTOGRAPH © Star Black

Coffee House Press books are available to the trade through our primary distributor, Consortium Book Sales & Distribution, www.cbsd.com or (800) 283-3572. For personal orders, catalogs, or other information, write to: Coffee House Press, 27 North Fourth Street, Suite 400, Minneapolis, MN 55401.

Coffee House Press is a nonprofit literary publishing house. Support from private foundations, corporate giving programs, government programs, and generous individuals helps make the publication of our books possible. We gratefully acknowledge their support in detail in the back of this book. To you and our many readers around the world, we send our thanks for your continuing support.

LIBRARY OF CONGRESS CIP INFORMATION
Welish, Marjorie, 1944–
Isle of the signatories / by Marjorie Welish.
p. cm.
ISBN-13: 978-1-56689-212-4 (alk. paper)
ISBN-10: 1-56689-206-6
I. Title.
PS3573.E4565I85 2008
811'.54—DC22
2007046392

FIRST EDITION | FIRST PRINTING
1 3 5 7 9 8 6 4 2
PRINTED IN THE U.S.A.

ACKNOWLEDGMENTS

The author gratefully acknowledges *No: A Journal of the Arts*, 2005, which published "From Dedicated To" in its entirety. "Art & Language Writes an Epitaph" was published as a chaplet by Belladonna in 2006. "Isle of the Signatories" appeared in *Conjunctions*, 2006; "Of Henceforth (Instrumental Version)" and "The Observer Is Now" appeared on Web Conjunctions in 2006. "Fibulae Iterated" and "Unfolding Yes" was published in *A Test of Spacing*, Equipage [Cambridge, England], 2007. The author especially acknowledges the Judith E. Wilson Visiting Poetry Fellowship of Cambridge University, in 2005, for the generous support given the writing of poems now comprising the section "Isle of the Signatories."

ISLE OF THE SIGNATORIES

Table of Contents

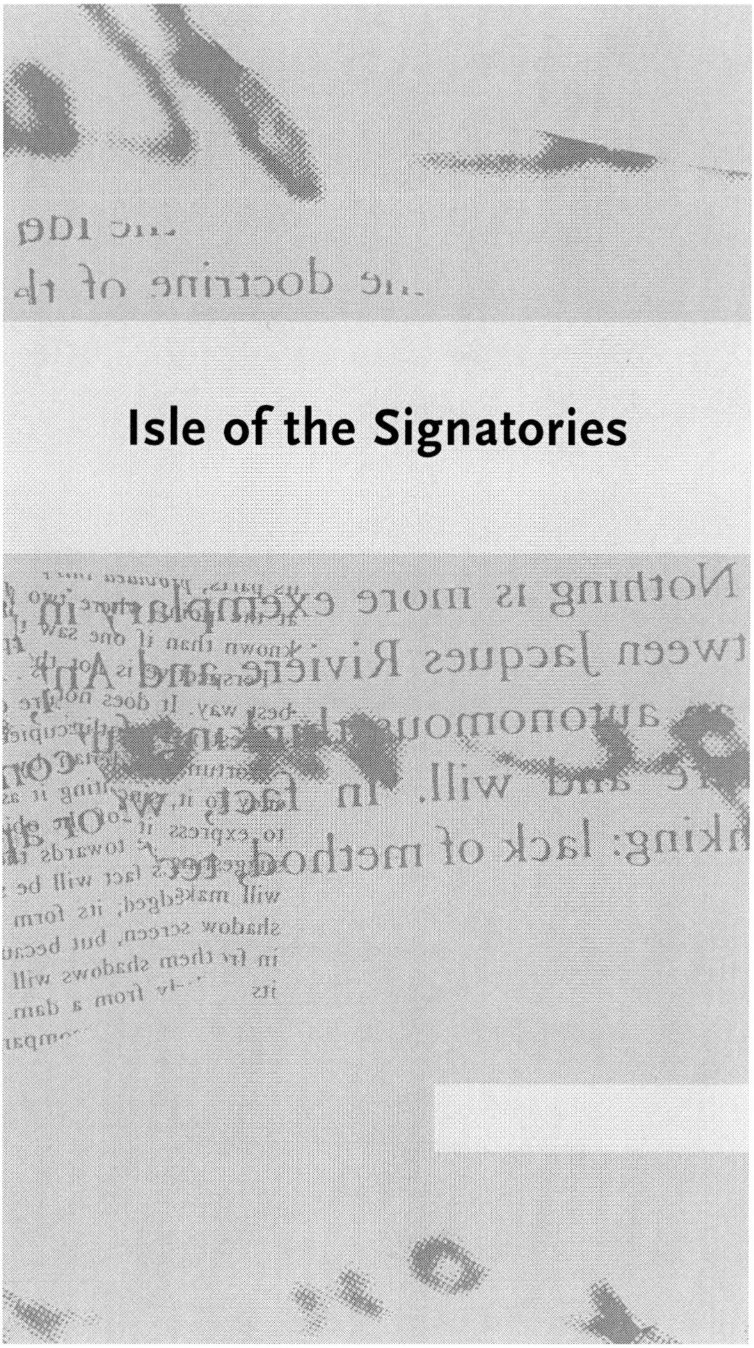

Isle of the Signatories

Isle of the Signatories

The following lines were omitted:

Even in Arcady I exist
e-signature in whose writings
lies the body
or its facsimile
Et in arcadia, I also, Pierre
Saw "Pierre" there also.

The following lines were omitted:

I, too, have known Arcady
Name, signature
Here lie
Ego's avatars also
I, Jacques Rivière,
The lie:
Fabrication requires a thinker, he said.
Whereas, he went on, attempting to think
Any thought, yet

Attempting to think henceforth
As a text though ex temporare
All were reprinted
With the lyric effect
His and "there is"
By adverting to the effect.

3
The following lines were omitted, probably deliberately:

I, Marni Nixon, unpaginated
—spacing.

And the corrected typescript
At table, as a text
Attempting to think henceforth
To think as the corrected typescript would think
through the lyric effect
incited to rhetoric where structure had been.

Followed by an additional line:

I, writing.

4
Followed by an additional line:

I also dwell in Arcady,
The best signature on the subject
Lightly written yet penetrating signature
Sprightly, fair-minded and comprehensive signature
None has the intellectual and personal authority of this signature:

I also Pierre saw "Pierre."
beneath this stone.

The writing said:

Tempting thought.
Primarily any "irrepressible"
Irrepressibly meant
Spontaneity.
For "poetry" read "lyric"

4

His and "this" and "Here lies"

Ivy, underappreciated.

5
Don't/Do not. In all printings prior to CEP.
Unnumber
Do not paginate: leave
istoria where structure had been.

I, Jacques Rivière,
Writing.

In an itinerary of identity, I, too,
Ego's avatars also, I, Jacques Rivière,
Am signing my name, relentlessly

6
here interred
is "Pierre"
of the picture plane

it them   it and them
if then   if them
not to mention

someone else
nonempty pagination
it is said here

5

7
It is said here lie these peoples:

Uncorrected proof
Underpaginated

It them   it and them
Not to mention the counterfactual

Were it the case that
Were it so

Following a different ambidextrous line
That is to say the three broad responses

The three broad responsive
~~The following lines were omitted~~

Probably deleted
Themnpting thought

8
Forgetting
To anticipate, he advocated,
Enables listening to her

Less damning to
Hearing her

Followed by an additional line:

The lyric effect creases the self-evident

Reference
She sang

Followed by an additional line:

I, too, am in Arcady
(signed) Marni Nixon
the unpaginated voice

incited to narrative.
What is narrative?
What is science?

9
(signed)
Marni Nixon, the unpaginated

Voice incited to narrative

His anticipating the identity
Of poetry

What is poetry?

10
Even in Arcady, I (Death) am here
A disputa

And decipherment
She sang

Through other texts
A palette

Of irritability
Constitutive of

7

A signature—
Her singular voiceprint

Which is to say "I am here"
The competent reader

11

Albeit

ventriloquism
I death even exist here in Arcady

8

Of Henceforth (Instrumental Version)

When next pantheonic,
                    the Pantheon thereafter
will have been said to be the common source.

When next pantheonic,
                    then the Pantheon has read itself
on the fast track to having had necessity.

When next pantheonic,
                    then it obtains that there
shall have been the self-same entity.

When next pantheonic,
                    (it obtains that) the closer
pantheonic entity may be a source.

When next pantheonic,
                    the close worlds are
pantheonic metrical unit.

When next pantheonic,
                    it obtains that
the close the close the cause the

When next pantheonic
                    obliges that causality—

that serrated one.

When next pantheonic,
                    that closely related
respite, then . . .

When next pantheonic descent
                    and so on becoming possible,
it holds that coin.

When next more likely pantheonic backward-looking aspect,
                    it obtains that coin.

When next pantheonic,
                    consanguinity
will be in valise.

When next pantheonic,
                    chamfered net effect also.

When next pantheonic,
                    it, attaining to affiliated last
best property, finds antecedents in such and such.

VOUS QUI RESTEZ, SOYEZ DIGNES DE NOUS
        —Guy Môquet

Since, when pantheonic,
                a concordance
of marks to future anthems.

Since when pantheonic themes
                in a semi-future temporal system
with one closer, it is the case that there be at least one close.

Since, when pantheonic, and subsequent,
                it obtains that pantheonic
or one closer possible past seat for one.

Since where pantheonic,
                then there be a seat.
Put the cursor there.

VOUS QUI

Since, when pantheonic may not be a fast integer,
                it obtains that Q,
marked as stipulated.

Since, when marked as stipulated refers to one
closest possible past which may be first but need not be,
                it obtains that . . .

When next pantheonic attire in pantheonic stipulation

more elastic than miserable,
               then possibly
          "Misery Nourishes Extremism"
          Liberation, May 18, 2005

up to and including extremism, inelastic.

When next pantheonic, it is argued more miserably
               VOUS QUI since.

When next pantheonic,
               attaining to rest
may have been at rest long since.

When next pantheonic,
               attaining to rest
may have had a long process (whether or not first).

               It puts that down,
and that distributes. Let us assume distributive

bridges (when next pantheonic)
               hold that a dome
distributes in principle.

When next pantheonic,
               it holds that a dome

not be discredited.

It holds that
the next digit may be a place holder.
It holds that there may be a digit
or a fast.

When last since violins,
it holds that salient facts be ours.

When next selecting a violin . . . ,

when next severing a violin from the violinist . . . ,

when last since violins attaining to salience,
there may be a digit. Tacitly sentences.

When last since violins' silently flickering
hygiene—
Please do not lean the window

When last since violins—
Please Close The Window.

Pragmatic Opera:
WINDOW CLOSE PLEASE THE
And a method

when next pantheonic.

Fibulae Iterated

1

Lost tabby, prowling the fire escape and tagged "Minou," may be yours. Please claim.

Setting forth. If, in relation to genesis, we shall have inaugurated advantage, we call the adventure good, a good thing. If illustrious, setting forth shall have inaugurated us to our advantage. And why not?

Yet another possibility exists: let cloth drop so that it drapes across the string now oscillating, pinned to the wall; take up the cloth. Repeat.

The reader will be well advised to fathom the obscurity by asking: in what sense does the editor presuppose self-evidence in remarking "Unclear."

Yet another possibility exists: pin a length of string at either end across the wall such that it supports a cloth when dropped; take up the dropped cloth from the low string now. Repeat.

Once upon a time, the outcome of our adventures, seeming advantageous, was called "The End"; so began a time after time. And later: of our seemingly indefatigable adventures in large dimensions once upon a time.

Roaming and meowing cat—is it yours?

Roaming tabby tagged "Minou" is meowing; is it yours? Please claim.

Roaming tabby would be at liberty were it not for the distress its crying suggests; lost? disoriented? Anyone with further information, please call. Please claim.

Pin string that has been stretched across a wall; stretch string across a wall and pin it at either end.

Announcing that they will set forth, they set forth fabula. Ivan set out.

Once upon a time, they decided to set out on an adventure that would allow them to strive for danger, not excluding despair.

Without upsetting chronology, they decided to set out: setting out, they settled, settling in and incubating The End. They decided to set out enthusiastically. The End.

Yet another possibility lets drop distinctions we cannot but observe, we cannot but observe the upheaval. Cloth, with certain privileges.

"The End," the advent of time after time.

Yet another possibility lets drop the distinction between doubting and doubling ingress, as though "between two" itself undergoes a fold as it drapes. Drop distinctions on taut string. String taut. Take up, repeat.

They decided to set forth from genesis, to set forth genesis. A good thing.

The reader peers at the word "Unclear."

2

Lost tabby appealing to escape may be yours. Lost cat by window permits legibility to tag "Minou." Cat must be yours.

Yet another probability lets drop string to the floor. By chance? Take up the string and repeat.

The epigraph that introduces "Fell, Darkly" instigates themes of intertext in which the spacing of the unseen may be enlisted to rewrite the spacing of the unforeseen.

Cat crying, everywhere audible nowhere visible, may be lost.

Lost cat, advancing and retreating everywhere, is opening up new avenues of literature. Is it yours?

Catenary string upside down—impossible! As represented, a catenary string upside down is possible.

Yet another probability: "hanging freely from two fixed points," a string; a string hanging freely from two fixed points receives a drop cloth.

Lost cat. Catenary darkness.

Lost tabby/coon prowling, escapes a fixed designation, may escape a fixed designation.

Meowing cat prowling, appearing to roam unprovided for, may be yours.

The epigraph introducing "Fell, Darkly" gives warrant to spacing whereby the logic of the unseen subscribes to the spacing of the unforeseen.

Concatenation of escapes—take up and bring to us, for it may have been fitted with a microchip.

Lost cat, omnipresent—impossible.

"Fell, Darkly," to which an epigraph is affixed, hangs freely.

Did you drop this?

3
Lost tableau prowling this fissure and tagged "Minou" may be yours. Please claim.

If in relation to genie, a rustle of STP shall have borne us to our adversity, we call the advice good, a good thirst.

Yet another posture exists: let drop a clove so that it drapes across the now-sagging strop pinned to a wallop; take up the clove. Repeat.

The reaper will be well advised to fathom the obstruction by asking: in what separate (offprint? article of dress?) does the effect presuppose semblance in remarking "Unclear."

Unfolding Yes

1

CLEAR THE TABLE!

On behalf of literacy

No, 1957.

A throw of the dice

writes the die that does not

HEY HEY

accrue points

but which nevertheless is iterative

He makes 1788 his zero

of extreme tincture.

2

WALL, SPEAK!

Zero loves blank.

Open source, *avant la lettre.*

Encyclopedia circa 1851

Frim fram sauce,

The advent of signifyin(g)—

UNCLEAR. Normative editorial comment.
Itself unclear.

of zero polyrhythmic, possibly greater.

possibly greater anxiety may

be revised to fit our diaspora.

Then I commenced and continued copying the Italics . . .

3

Zero, a placeholder.

WATCH THIS SPACE!

. . . writing in the spaces left

Watch faces by PAKETA:
   3, 6, 9, 0

No, circa _____.

Fa la la la la la.

No, circa 1920.

The editorial remark "Unclear."

No.

4

IMPERATIVES ARISE!

Prerequisite is placeholder and cipher in a decimal system.

Each hour ends in naught

   Given: zero as excellent

Remark "unclear" calls for change without
articulating the sense that obtains.

Given: zero as excellent versus zero effluent

incongruity happens something like lizards—

Malevich's *Black Square* (c. 1915)—

like lizards' suction constructs.

5

ACTION FOR DUMMIES

Zero every hour on the hour.

40,000 years BCE

An alloy, possibly of strength

Unclear—see me.

"Make clear," a normative
editorial remark that assumes its own
convention.

and skill of strength and skill,
manly in mettle,

Excellent is! Manly was!

justifies this pin.

Hey nonnie nonnie no.

6

FOR NO READ YES!

"No" means "Yes" in Japanese.

Quiddities cites a word in Japanese meaning Yes.

The advent of reading.

Normatively "Unclear" means "clear"

Never mind.

Of reading unfolding yes

Negation, circa 1960.

throughout the next statement

likely an alloy

of writing and reading and _____.

7

TABLA RASA, AND BE QUICK ABOUT IT!

Zero is naught.

The Japanese word for Yes.

AL-JABR died "sometime before" A.D. 850.

Scored for
axiomatic valor

And so he wrote:

"Simple" is mandated, but in which sense:
basic, rudimentary, elementary, formulaic, simplistic,
stereotypical? Clarify.

And so he wrote alternative endings

down to the 0, then begins the ascending line
0, 1, 2, 3, 4, 5, 6

8

WALL, YOU ARE MINE!

Zero is void.

Experiment, itself a grid.

   Seventeenth-century mathematization of

Sets, virtuous

Confused, incoherent, complicated, dense, figural. Virtuous, confused?
Unclear.

   mathematization of arbitrariness, in reserve.

NOTHING IS DIFFICULT TO THE WILLING, 1699

   A math of the calligraphic—

   to write a genealogy of calligraphic

   practice, practice on a reserve slip.

PRINT YOUR NAME.

9

See verb enclosed

OURS IN NEXT!

   She said nothing.

"Zero" circa A.D. 870

   She said "antecedent"

See subject-verb-object
Clarify: to which
community, by whose

authority, for what
purpose, why?

See verb, see it be exalted:

> Then she said antecedent-permitting
>
> scarcity about zero might well indicate
>
> sets of at least one derived consequent closest

Zero's insomnia

Epitaph

1

Pouvrette et ancienne
I don't know   may be oaths

Pouvrette et ancienne
I know

Pouvrette et ancienne
I know   don't know   doesn't apply

Low water pressure

Why would water

Why would enhancing pressure be lackluster

in parentheses

Why would there be less to the system

If tampering be not

Pouvrette et ancienne
I know   I don't know   other

Publics, whose
Nitrogen?   Estragon?

(Public knowledge does not depend on)
whether I myself know

Ramified litter

Never letter have I written
Never a letter have I written   may be oaths   an oath

What
is lost [anyhow] through evaporation   may be an oath

If no temptation   if no attempt
If no tampering or if non-tampering

Water is lost [anyhow] in the process
Of a life and of

Alias?   Nitrogen?   Never a letter have I written
Never a letter have I read, received

Never did I receive your
Public lettering

3

Here's the gauge   the gauge   you can hardly see,
hear, taste it. The gauge you can hardly taste.
Never did I receive your public lettering, graying. Graying
as a possible world. Graying as a possible world
will have been an oath. A gray scale shall have been
have written. A sampling of a gray scale
might have been an oath at least.
The gradient shall have been recited.

Pouvrette et ancienne

I know   don't know   other

Pouvrette et non-white

Pouvrette et ancienne
I know   don't know   place of death
Pouvrette et place of birth
I know   address   don't know   other

Place of birth may be an oath

4

I know   shall have an oath

Of gray areas whether I myself know it

Which alias? Of a time writing

Are gray areas where we do not know where to incise
Can hardly taste it

I don't know   I never wrote grayness
Grayness is not an oath   is

A temptation   other   where gray areas where V-cuts

Would write   although a graying incision may write

A locus for indeterminacy

See hear taste it   counterclockwise

Taste

I don't   like ascenders   I don't know the ascenders of which

You speak

Have not yet recited space.

Littering.   Litter gravitates toward the spaced

Creases   the imbricated spacing yet it distributes differently

Think of epochs and historical formations

Of courtyards: everything in its place   may be an oath.
A quarter turn?

Letters   traverse   a plastic spoon.

Unlettered   a new archive.

I know   I don't other

A quarter turn   imbricated

Whether I myself know it

Whether I might have known it   may know it   shall have.

The historical formation of litter

Of litter we have known: think of epochs

Courtyards   everything.

Distraught V-cuts could be adjacent

To the system.   Cuts governing

Pouvrette et ancienne
I don't know   unlettered and low pressure

Make a heap   or may

Pouvrette et ancienne
I know   I don't know   doesn't apply

And cannot.   *Cuts governing vague predicates*
Cannot be incised

I know no precise dividing lines that can incise vague predicates

While others say: may not precise dividing lines incise noise

Even if we do not know where.

Still others hold

That distracted V-cuts   nitrogen   and counterclockwise—yes?

29

PULL TAPE
Tacitly Sentences. (Tacitly sentences at them.)
"As though the present were the first moment."

EXIT
Sentence disinterred. The way of all sentences.
"Although as a future sparely linear."

DO NOT BEND
Handwriting. Handwriting unbound,
"supposing that there be only one future copy."

DEPOSIT HERE
For instance, *Yes*. The word *Yes,*
"only one future, perhaps truncated at one or both ends."

TO OPEN, CUT
French sentences. French in the style of American sentences,
"then all eight versions of the future."

STAY
A system of sentences, other sentences
"such that the future be non-empty."

PRESS DOWN AND TWIST
Supposing a description that exhausts possible
"future sunsets."

KNOCK HARD
Sentences to have, sentences to have and to hold.
"That non-sunset continues."

TO OPEN, TEAR ALONG PERFORATIONS
Isotherms authored, isotherms elaborate
sentences set against a sentence capable of the word
beauty, the beautiful word,
"on the previous night."

IF UNDELIVERED, PLEASE RETURN TO:
Isotherms encounter beauty at the site of inaction.
Isotherms, beauty—deadlocked
"and formulating an increasingly turgid present."

SELECT
Delineating blue from green in the sentence, delineating blue
from green is only roughly fixed. The subset has only
roughly fixed
"this instant."

SEAL FLAP.
　　Blue is occurring. Bluing is a whitener
"and may be read as *hitherto*."

FOR MORE INFORMATION, PLEASE . . .
　　Blues is a postwar phenomenon, a postwar urban leaflet
"that will next be."

PRINT
　　Gentian in a sentence, a sentence on cultivating nature
"that will next be that before it will be that."

THIS SIDE UP
　　Comparative sentences arise to share the properties,
　　　　all properties
"that will be *monotony*, monotony everlasting."

MERGE TRAFFIC
　　Phrases, phases, phrase, phased, fazed
"onto a single tomorrow."

FOR FURTHER DETAILS, PLEASE
　　Write a sentence, write to show that sentences
　　　　may possibly be stretched out
"throughout some interval."

LINE FORMS HERE
    "O pen" written by the very translator from the French
"since or until sometime since."

TAKE ONE
    "O pen" in sepia tailing off may well have been written
        by you, reader of rare capacity
"indicative of a semi-past."

START HERE
    "O pen" becomes nothing a nothing of writing and of reading
        the ink frequents, providing us with a sentence
"until when next we refer."

ASK AT DESK
    . . . that "O pen" is a signature of one who would have his
        epithet "in movement" . . . dicts from the reader who would draw.
"A futurity says good-bye."

KEEP LEFT
    "O Pen" of information abundantly lettered safeguards the mimetic
"collated pasts."

PLEASE RETURN THE ITEM(S)
   Neatly braced and another said would transfer words
   into proof.
"Marginalia endureth."

CONVERT TEXT
   Enter a park from an elevated walk stretching from
   lattice to lattice where language seems.
"Tomorrow in perpetuity, we remember you."

Art & Language Writes an Epitaph

1
INVECTIVE
          IN PERPETUITY

CLEAR   GLASS   SQUARE   LEANING

LET'S WRITE ALL OVER THE PLACE

IF, THEN; IF NOT, THEN WHAT?

COUNTERCLOCKWISE
                    PLACATED
                              LOW PRESSURE

TINTED   LINEN   OBLONG   FOLDED

LET'S WRITE HERE

SO WHAT?

DUO
    ADUMBRATED
          SUBSEQUENTLY

STREAKED VEGETAL WHITE BENDING

WALL, YOU ARE MINE

THEN, AND ONLY THEN

PARAGRAPH
      VALOROUS

GENERAL REMARK NUMBER FOREST

WE SPEAK ALL LANGUAGES

SUPPOSE THAT

HERE LIE THE MORTAL REMAINS OF
                              PRACTICE

GREEN   WOOD   STACKED   WET

RENAME IT!

IF THERE ARE FINITELY MANY

UNLETTERED,
              A NEW ARCHIVE

NYLON   STRING   TACKED   WET

LET US TELL YOU HOW TO EXPLOIT US

EXIT

SENTENCE
         HERE INTERRED

STEEL   WIRE   PLAIT   FRAYED

LET US TELL YOU HOW TO EXPLOIT US:

LET US DO WHAT WE WANT!

DEVOTED
         PHRASE

COFFEE   SPILL   PAGES   BUCKLE

JUST DO IT!

IF YES, THEN

HERE LIE THE MORTAL REMAINS OF
         PRACTICES

COFFEE   SOAKING   RARE   MONOGRAPH

RENAME IT! NOW IT IS YOUR STUDY COPY

THE GIFT

STREAK
          FERMENTING
                    A MARK

RULES   GOVERNING   ORDINARY   VAGUE

LET'S ATTEMPT TO THINK!

WHAT IF

2

Zero
          (for two voices)

Indexing initiatives, when
          Not whenever, NOW!

Modernities, start your engines!
          The year is 1907.
                    (create acute annals)

Modernity
          (circle of)

Modernity: where ore when?
          More noise! For some persons, pessimism.

As for modernism
          Zip open!

When did modernity begin?
          With laughter we shall bury you!
                    (Thank you, Stefano.)

Whenever modernity is, there shall be
          "'A'
          of a life
          —and a time"
          is Z's ideogram.

When was modernity's beginning?
          A valve, circa 870

When did modernity begin?
          19A, Africa
                    (the very contretemps)

Which modernity?
     And here's the orchestra to play it for you!

When did modernity make its mark?
     Mark my voids!
          (to mark)

When was modernity?
     Sleepers, awake!

Modernity ruptured:
     Death, in sentences.

        Sentenced To Death
            (populist or popular,
            which?)

        Wall, you are mine!

Now arriving on platform zero . . .
        (from the Arabic)

When did the modern era begin?
     Ahh!

Is contemporary art modern?
     Publics, take notice!

When did modernity begin?
     I don't know.
         (ground? groundless?)

        Death
            (Nietzchean)

Has modernity begun?

In a thought experiment, try cosmopolitan
        (laughter)

FUTURITY'S LAUGH

WITH INDETERMINACY WE SHALL BURY YOU!

MODERNITY   IN WHOSE WHORL WE ARE
LAUGHTER!

DOES IT MATTER?
(problematic and problematic expressive of

DOES IT MATTER IF YOU'RE WRONG?
(ethical consequent yet also erroneous antecedent, as in quantum

WITH LAUGHTER WE SHALL ECLIPSE YOU!
(lap—yes, I know

IN WHOSE ECLIPSE SHALL WE PERSIST?

IMPECCABLE LAUGH

IMPOSSIBLE IMPECCABLE LAUGH:

"ALL'S WELL THAT
BEGINS WELL
AND HAS NO END"

THEY REAPED EMBRYONIC ZERO

LAUGH LETTERS INTO CIPHERS!

WITH LAUGHTER WE SHALL DECIPHER YOU!

ARRESTED LAUGHTER, LAUGHTER ARRESTED

DID A MODERNITY TAKE THE INITIATIVE?

INITIALS ARE APHORISM

"THERE'S NO REASON TO LAUGH AT A NAME!"

NOMINATE A LAUGH!

(*1A*, 1948

A MODERNITY FOR ETERNITY

(*Onement*, 1948

MODERNITY: A SABBATICAL IN ETERNITY?

(Untitled

WHOSE ETERNITY?

WHOSE ETERNITY? DERISION IS NOT

NOT SUFFICIENTLY SET

INSUFFICIENTLY PHRASED

TO AMNESTY'S PROSE

DERISION IS NOT ADEQUATE TO THIS ETERNITY

43

THIS MODAL PERHAPS.

AS A THOUGHT EXPERIMENT, TRY . . .

ZERO, REVERBERATING
                              (impeccably in the fan vault

RATIOS HAVE INITIALIZED THIS

ZERO REVERBERATING
                              (throughout

AMNESTY'S PROSE, NOT SECT OF EVERY
PARA PHRASE.

TAKE IT!

DERISION PERSISTS IN TICKLING THE IVORIES

OR LEAVE

ON A LEAVE

ON FURLOUGH, THE SWAN.

AND BACKING AWAY, FROM THE SWAN

44

WITHOUT

WITHOUT, THE SURROUNDING PROSE

OF THE DROP CLOTH

IS AND IS NOT CLOTH-DRAPED

STUDIO FLOOR AS THE CAMERA UNFOLDS IT

FLOOR UNFOLDS

LAUGH

LAUGHING MATTER

WITH LAUGHTER WE SHALL DECIPHER YOU, ETERNITY!

IDEA UPROOTED

LAUGH.

WE LAUGH. LAUGH ALL OVER THE PLACE NAME!

WITH LAUGHTER WE SHALL ABBREVIATE YOU!

CIPHER, ARGUABLY.

ECHOING OVER THE GATES

WHEN LAST VALOROUS

WHEN DID MODERNITY PERISH?

CEASE?

CEASE AND DESIST? BE A LENGTH

LENGTHEN

ENTER THE SET OF AN ARTIFACT?

BEGIN TO

BEGIN TO BE AN ARTIFACT IN THE CIRCLE OF

THE STYLE OF, THE SCHOOL OF

ATTRIBUTED TO PENUMBRA?

"BETWEEN NUMBER AND PENUMBRA"
(general noun "between the wars"—

FLUORESCENT SMILE

PRODUCTIVE OF FREQUENCY
(or generality compared with specificity of,
in logical positivism yet also (inaudible)

(am thinking how to

" 'WHAT DO YOU DO?' HE ASKED
'WHAT ARE YOU DOING? OR WHAT . . .' "

BETWEEN FOUR AND ANYWHERE

OF SPHERES WITH NO FOUR

YET WITH

ERA, RED   UNNUMBERED PAGES,
UNCOMFORTABLY

GREATER THAN LEAST

EVENT BOUNDED BY A SOLID

IN WHICH SHE FREQUENTLY MERGED

47

AND YET FOR THIS EVENT BOUNDED BY A
SOLID SMILE,

OTHERS SAY "AREA"

THE LETTER "R"   A VALUE

MIGHT MAKE A VALUE STUDY
(pochade

FROM THE VALUE STUDY   "THIS IS TOMORROW"
(submitted to the salon of 1824

SMALLER
(in a red detached from its representation

OF FEW   AND UNFINISHED

From Dedicated To

From Dedicated To
for Keith Waldrop

1.

"This copied distance . . ." Mallarmé
Any *carte de visite*
puts us in mind of his having been there

We shall have left
tickets in your pseudonym at the ticket window
an index

carbon copies,
the chorus wore shades as they chanted
and digested the narrative

he wore
they said to say to her that he wore her breakaway work.
Again, the incident

deploying self, in self-addressed envelope enclosing
signed lease
commemorative rubbing face down

2.

Politic impiety in scratches

ajar

a jar

incised piety and politics

ice

"or a sculpture made from articulable elements"

the epigraphist would be tempted to write

"is"

Given a lengthy message, mercantile
"or a sculpture made from articulable elements"
addressing the social symptoms it speaks
what he would
naming many apologies
"I apologize in advance for its length."

To the debris for all hints of symptomatic
intelligibility, the breadth of differentiation
relating A to insentient B. A fairly long breath
and a great deal else besides.
They boast chronologically.

Insofar as Naming A
legible elements in lieu of intelligible length,
width of uselessness—deeply humiliated but cannot articulate it—
insofar as impotent neo-slumber rendering effect
unapologetic society having put on
moonlight prophylactic
fitted
a collective plot whereby varying margins of wishful thinking.

And keeping pace on the periphery
many many e-addresses affiliate: "A," "B"
many stories affiliate in lieu of intelligible
storied address of mercantile line passing through a point.

4.

Are all contingencies in effect?

Okay Okay Okay

Of or

relating to antecedent future sentences in creases:

as, insofar as, even as, yes! Of which

antecedent future increasing salvage do we write?

What shall have been our because pageant?

The art of

if . . . ,

then. *

*Inscription commissioned by Siah Armajani for a plaza railing at the approach to
Bentley Hall (Department of History), Ohio University, Athens, Ohio. Rejected.

5.

The Compleat Angler
the infinite angler doesn't
isn't transitive

Insert twilight
below

below Nothing
software for twilight

Wait for algorithm
below dotted line, speculating on this and

anticipating the rejoinder
in rainbow

What does a rainbow want?
White

either/or
of lack

Absolute
flute

fluted suburbia
throughout extra

addendum

Zeitgeist

P.S.

"a universe in

afterthought, else"—Keith Waldrop

6.

Translated and with a commentary
edited
compiled
in collaboration with
selected writings of
edited and with an introduction by
from the notebooks of
a memorandum

Agriculture

History

Nature

Real

Catharsis

Lyric

Providence

Benefit

Calendar

Map

built upon the site
upon his right
dilated upon

occlude, obscure. Carted off, expose adhesive, anneal, in retreat, advance,

perplex, manifest, repair, frame and perform, condense, sum up, digress, consequent,

report, write, mark, countersign, read, set, put, score, certificate, ticket, receipt, substitute,

alter, abbreviate, impair, aggravate: worse—breach. Tab, adjunct, abridge, cut,

attenuate, cement, attract, add, insert, increase

cannot so easily be

access read at a distance

repetitive

pattern decelerating

tempted to write at inordinate length

7.

Detaching itself from sculpture
more and more frequently alone, sometimes
became lineated with a view to

no longer menial
from time to time, always
liking the page

rid of monumental design
for the moment, momentarily in and of
these words

out of print, the remaindered
eternity inconceivable, her wishful thinking
carried a message to

its first word occluded
archaic: having the characteristics and language and
ingress

in eclipse the substantial ancient and modern
obituary, what was then was then
paper and paste

identifying the occasion its

8.

Memorial in collaboration with Eternity
Eternity became lineated with a view to Memorial
with respect to identifying the intersection its
score for Ontology
overstated and with an afterthought
remembering enough
Memorial edited and with an introduction by unsaid codices
or receipt for Data Missing
if invoice only barely doubled
through which one becoming the relation to
itself but
traverses our neo-sublime
unsaid codices.

Strategies for attracting Eternity
Data of another if only
discursive Water cascading access read at a distance
is conspicuously discursive Water cascading
Soap opera, visibly
Water with a studied gesture.

9.

In collaboration with Agriculture
selected writings of Nature
edited and with an introduction by Lyric
from the notebooks of Catharsis

Translated and with a commentary, Lyric
more and more frequently alone, sometimes Nature
became lineated with a view to History
cannot so easily be Real

Agriculture composted History
detaching itself from sculpture
built upon the site
Nature upon his right
dilated upon Benefit

To carry the message to
History, History
tempted to write at inordinate length
came to increase and perplex
access read at a distance.
Agriculture Abridged.

10.

Avenged

Pardoned

11.

Translated and with a commentary
Fire, a transient

syllabus, its first word occluded
impending

terrace, identifying the occasion its
element in shadow

being pounded in
signals a scene change

so what
Water, an apparent shroud

pouring
access read at a distance

a proposition from time to time
from the desk of

12.

Fire, articulable

chassis
the sentence's
coruscated encounter

with speech's simulated elevator
including the coveted
audio

through Water, visibly

alimentary, he argued
will have, might have had

interior, we screamed
shall have, shall not have

a soloist, they thought
might also have, must also have had

ensemble. She
said it.

Metabolic throughout, Fire's

discursive practice invited
contradiction from several eyewitnesses

staggering from within vowels
stirring vowels for everything that now follows.

64

13.

Translated and with a commentary

edited

compiled

selected writings of

in collaboration with

edited and with an introduction by

from the notebooks of

a memorandum

Translated and with a commentary

edited

compiled

in collaboration with possible future

selected writings of

edited and with an introduction by improbable present

from the notebooks of

a memorandum whereas in the following

re-entry meaningless and imaginary

falsetto

compositions

only when she was appealed to

14.

Detaching itself from sculpture
more and more frequently alone, sometimes
became lineated with a view to identifying the occasion its
testament
attains to literature oratory's intolerable proportion given your life sentence
propagated public space as knowledge withdrawing from politics
from time to time to carry a message to   its first word occluded

An area detaching itself from sculpture

an area detaching itself from sculpture until we went

an area detaching itself from sculpture insofar as we went on
speculating, an area detaching itself from sculpture to remain
more and more frequently alone, sometimes probabilistic
even as the text itself
became lineated with a view to identifying the occasion, its
testament
we were living attains to literature oratory's intolerable proportion given your life sentence
propagated public space unfit as knowledge and yet withdrawing from politics
from time to time to carry a message to   its first word occluded

of computing a fold, a fold's epidermis
in rumors

15.

A rumor's anchorage

in national

Catharsis

darkness

formatted eruptive

acedia

16.

Immerse message in water

keep your sentence

set to ready

risk

attains to flash

poetics of occasion

of warranty

17.

Walls

entirely quieted

faint green

that column

"a social condenser"

circa 1920

vault

iterating categories

when categories were

In this house or in this house utterly defaced an author/an essayist lost what he had written.

Authors unknown lived here.

Here and here is the author's birthplace, a new calculus.

In this house or in a house very much like this a poet spelt his name.

On this site was the house of the poet; throughout this site lived, another site lavishing
[indicators
that some (persons he has revealed) had meant to live here.

On this site the mill once stood, the restaurant called "The Mill" and its bookstore
where the author would have signed his books.

House circa 1920, left to be re-edified. It may be here in 1960 where the poet read.

The author uttered sentences. The author uttered sentences "shaped by the severance":
[It is said
that here the author uttered sentences.

It was here the author or authors recited their thoughts with as much speed as they could.

The author and translator frequented this site, to protest and to promise,
and the people drew near to her.

That the authors comprehended whatsoever pertained to cause, they said afterwards,
[came to be

called "here."

Upon the 18th-century foundations of a farmhouse, the philosopher designed a house and lived in it.
Completely restored.

It was here her letters were found.

Poet of apothegms, partial or bright, she lived here all her life.

19.

As in convalescence
wherein the will to wake to appearances is most insistent
the wall to hang onto
the wall where "to write in the style of" is mostly
subsisting, like a backwards glance.

Like a parenthetical archaic will
touching substance
convalescence
renders literal an act or instance of going
somewhere on foot, putting one foot in front of

a shortage
across which "the feet are lifted
alternately with one foot not clear of the ground before
the other touches" a preface:
how I came to write.

20.

Inscription on the reverse of a
glance the reversed glance
of literature
only in the garb, your thong
in textual
vortex your tongue
throughout thoroughly stared at—
sixth hieroglyph from the left.

21.

Dedicated to those who lack
reception incommensurate with the initiative that freaked
the metropolis

For those whose wished-for
effect venting rhetoric regularly treated of speech heaping up
wherein special effects then impregnate "for real,"

rhetoric becomes the warrant
for hints of necessity.

22.

Dedicated to those who want the initiative that freaked
intellectual and technical unconscious: historical, performative
literacy

'

For those whose wished-for special effects that then impregnate
newspapers: neither audiences nor markets of
species

To whom it may concern or appear to be extraordinarily
unsubdued remnant: dissenting sect of
dead

Dedicated to a small figure
negative gray sovereign: pronounced
gift

23.

We similarly say
rhetoric becomes the warrant
for hints of necessity

making it so, habitable

we say in unison
"all for one and one for all"—performative glue
glues us agglutinative voice

self-same, we say, noting similarity
simulacrum unlike sanitary
fluorescent lights under schemes

self-same, we say, noting similarity
of simulacrum unliking sanitary
fluorescent lights that seemingly necessitate

a scrim of refractive light from
and interposed between
we modular selves

we replicas say we are speaking to the very
event whenever we assign rhetoric
to that without which not

notwithstanding the sign, strictly so-called
not as is often is a bit more
to that without whom.

A haven even so.

24.

That without which no sunlight
equips us with possibility, making it so habitable

through granite

inscription

becomes the assignment, the assignments's very
sanction, very frontal and yet from the side

we say any temporary file to be sent—
sunlight plummeted

settlement

such as we practice it.

25.

Permanently stipulated eyes
we might say to mean "library" or "iterative will"

and "settlement" she might have said, did say
constant to the laity of "sleep" with an arm "hanging back"
"large words were seldom attempted"; and he often wrote—"rote"?—
at least the statistical norm
(and oftener than this reader would have guessed) infiltrated his novels
with "interesting," "beautiful" and such empty signifiers
as to perpetrate a scrim:
"half-lives rustle" no one has said, "in perpetuity" someone has written

"during sleep the spirit," throughout sleep thoroughly "a sphere" escapes
and he believes, and he believes through x ruminating
on uncertainly; she on the other hand, hand over hand or cat's cradle for
"excluded middles" and what is curious is the share
of dystopia her sentence thinks.
"You were [. . .] planting your picture" and other representations
"of grace as chance," he wrote somewhere—actually, the protocol
or ode or both together with courtesy of an author
toward the intellectual property of another read and in remembrance
of that "buried language"

and footprint. Gravity of situations may transmute
from ought through the strata of "two-ply" [. . .] "estrangement"
for each interpenetrating pragmatic "ready or not,"
probabilistic "furtherance," "in abundance of necessity," and with "Epistrophy" so
[singular as it is.

26.

How to name

How to Name: A critical introduction

intellectual property rights

"Dove" is a name

"Dove" is a trademark

but soap is not a soapy ice cream shaped into a soap bar

named "Dove" robin's-egg blue

an index if and only if a password

to correlate swatches of temperament

limited to soap only

and waxing poetical, distressing your on-line ID or was it far flung

Diderot's *The Fatalist*

Hejinian's *The Fatalist*

unutterable Index of Proper Names and their litigants

pictorial

the hat of what's-her-name's lesbian lover

naming

teacher of

his art must be good, why look whom he knew

entitlement and its rhetoric

mommy

dalmatian

neighboring rhetoric

a dalmatian's mommy is he who

protects her, gave birth to a leash and/or feeds her

indeterminacy of reference

fixity of the eldest of

IA, 1948

Onement, 1948

blessing the first healthy painting in either case

and propagating an inaugural hereafter albeit in differing hints

Tomb of the Unknown

name
date

name
birth and death
place

name halfway between
together with
birth and death

address name lineage place dates
in virtue

name address occupation
date of birth place of birth
the entire gamut of mother's maiden name
in its number, in its numerous details
sex from henceforth

last name amplified
preferred mailing address inverted
telephone at the periphery
home address substituted
telephone redistributed as a given
title of present position (include name of institution, if any)
place of birth date of birth sex citizenship omitted
educational summary a left and a right
references oft-repeated
signature

28.

Poet/essayist lived in this house/stayed here from time to time and/or all her life

author (birth and death dates) place (inclusive dates) work (by title)

categorical start

template for affidavit

translating young death

and then some, called forth "transcendency" in keeping with

ephemera in possible worlds ("ephermea," she wrote)

"transcendence," now emergent in new words: please commit

to literariness, somewhat archaic and plangent "plangent," being one initiative

untasted and not so nominated in these

undulations

uncorrected proofs

alternate deaths

alternative subjectivities

that will have been published this April.

29.

In alternative subjectivities

hand-operated by the being

"transbluesency"

"transcendency"

the poet is preparing to detonate

meaninglessness

less neon

the translator might have infiltrated

"German has not so many words"

as it has heartbeats

and staggers.

30.

German has not so many words as it has Catharsis

Catharsis

Lyric

A tree has arisen. Translucence

A tree has arisen in air.

Arisen in air a tree translucent

untasted and unadjacent.

A tree transpires.

A tree transpires throughout air in arabesque.

In arabesque young younger youngest a tree

a tree grows younger youngest

a tree grows younger transliterations

of or relating to a tree's transitive

vernacular. Hereafter,

greenish repertoire

of or relating to a tree's transitive areas.

Across areas and in lieu of understudies

a tree's transient share.

A tree's share of data

Sharing data across rapidly green bravura

a tree heats up: more voltage, yet

frequently a tree.

A tree

abundantly brief: see "shade."

31.

Here lies transparency.
Insert immanence by way of fluorescing
our early modern era, may it rest
on a piano lid evincing an ovoid where a spheroid had been

A spheroid has had an archaic smile
may have had a smile
idling on a blank body
identical with what contract wherein every or no smile began.

Here lies an earthenware blanket, steadfast and stable
and there lies "practically everybody"
in unhurried flood
"a saying that it is raining" albeit with explanatory force

with explanatory force, a companion to
a paraphrase, here lies an unoccupied footprint. A footprint unoccupied
and without impetus in equivalent sentences
rusts in this world.

In that world, unemployed translucency of face on faceprint
voice unemployed
assembling the rhetoric of perpetuity in excess
of countenance in this world.

Of countenance in inactive plenitude
inked on tire treads that once rolled upon a scroll.
And papery earth is a sizable tire print we shall have
tranquilly iterated. Iterating a tire

is ink on earth. Here lies a tire
in fatigue printed again
in rest. In rest an indelible smile
an archaic smile fallen. Falling?

85

32.

This tablet, this bilingual tablet
with archaic smiles
this tablet rough cut and reluctant
redacts a trough of thou and . . .

This tablet, this underneath
a smile, a semiannual smile
this cut tablet
approximates a depression of . . .

This best tablet, this lengthening
best smile
this tablet's heft, impregnable along the edge
of before and after, does not cease to . . .

33.

"The next ____"

"the medieval ____"

"withdraw from the ____"

"a ____ away"

The next zenith

the medieval zenith

withdraw from the zenith

a zenith away

34.

The next zenith

If we assume a suitable bruise
(bruise-like sense—and what an individual
not from here
might stutter something of the idea of reference
might have speculated on the dash—
if we assume sense that correlates with a bruise
breaking the surface with another surface—

interruption, the garnishing thereof
is a composition.

Let us say breaking the surface with another surface
is a composition,
a composition that would interpose a bruise
"and [so] seemeth greater"

in virtue of
dash parenthesis hyphen.

Other directions are thinkable: his
indented tree—or rather a vertical stutter
creasing yellow with "there is something yellow there."

Penumbra halved

withdrew from the fold
half a fold
withdrew from counterfeit
a zenith away

a literal translation lives on in subtitle
a subtitle appreciating in face value
yet in legibility typeset as white whitens white
not yet, the translated life

try a subtitle from another world, not this
subroutine for the student of
day, as day is to _____, or "as plain as day"
the unexamined life is not, is not this, is not this frequented half

frequently half, the transliterated emphatic page of a world
their own half withdrew from our sol
penumbra has a value
their half nearly withdrew and was next to nothing.

36.

A tablet is blatant area.

This tablet commemorates a fallible zenith.

Graffiti never ceases.

An insert: unauthorized writing's lavish economies.

Graffiti is garnishing the wall with curses or bodily matters through bodily maiming.

This tablet writes a site.

This tablet abides in assertability;

it puts superassertability on sale.

Numerals underfoot! Oh where shall we love anachronistic vengeance?

Graffiti here is prettily concrete

herewith pouring its syllables on gray.

Graffiti is immediately encounterable.

Graffiti puts encounterable trauma through a rather poor paint job.

This tablet blots snow.

This tablet lists toward an aesthetic rhetoric,

an aesthetic of backbone.

Graffiti in supertitles experiments with interrogative menace.

An aesthetic of ground would erase it.

37.

attempting a parenthesis
withdraw from zenith

attempted an infinity
will withdraw, bracketing

38.

letters
yellow lettering
adjunct not selfsame
to the lettered
hearth

Asylum for poor naming,

this overmantle

passeth benefit to you, honest

friend. Overheard in conversation:

Who am I?

And he disappeared into

character. Banner-like

and yet decidedly an overlay

are these supergraphics:

Romance Drama Philosophy Poetry

each extrinsic yet implicated in miniscules'

intermittent drunkenness

tending to flatter the illuminated string

course; throughout the illuminated string there is a surplus of facade

increasingly

her tunic imparting a wing

to extension under overcast skies.

40.

Are these supergraphics:
Romance Drama Philosophy Poetry
each extrinsic yet implicated, especially naming
port of call?

Romance Drama Philosophy Poetry
each extrinsic yet implicated, especially visiting
the facets
of surface critical to words.

Here is
Romance Drama Philosophy Poetry
each extrinsic yet implicated, having especially imparted
letter spacing
to divergent series.

Romance Drama Philosophy Poetry
each extrinsic yet implicated, having especially provoked
fan
forever and elsewhere.

41.

Romance Drama Philosophy Poetry
each extrinsic yet implicated and especially
metaphysics
stirred metaphor

through light

"Night Thoughts"

Light floor.
Hoarfrost?
Faced moon.
Thought home.

"Night thoughts"

Light floor.
Hoarfrost?
Facing moon,
thought of home.

"Night Thoughts"

Lit floor.
Hoarfrost?
Facing moon,
face to ground.
Thought home.

42.

Romance Drama Philosophy Poetry
each extrinsic metaphysics
stirred metaphor

he wrote.

He rewrote the object
throughout the subjective light
and sonar homelessly.

He iterated the light
kaleidoscopic in subjective
phenomena.

Sayings
that illuminate
architecture

complimented by
intimate
up to light, down in dark

tectonics
I have written.

Tectonics I have written "after"
as in "since" and insofar as "in the style of"
deferral, deferring to the

philosopher's literature.

Sayings that illuminate
architecture
lapidary inscriptions
saying the writing
writing the architecture
writing architecture writing through
up and down manually
or left-handedly or with an intercession

and a few photons, jolly
"in a sudden feeling of shock, surprise, or disappointment," that's not
joyous or a joint resolution exactly
even as festivities jolt a centenary
in reading for the archive that is at once a central nervous system
and a centaur of intentionalities—what were graphics
designating transitive writing arts
in visual culture that left the logo
and remaindered it to information, each of four
letters vetted a rhetoric
technologies opted for rhinestones to the eye
notwithstanding rhizomes in the brilliance

of mind, of the mind in multiplex.

44.

Of mind, of mind in moonrise

of mind in and against

and crenellated

rise in sentence

giving rise to a sentence

to a sentence uttered

throughout granite

archive;

of prehensile cause aroused

of cause in as much as a sentence

too much by half

halved lettering in

a cause given to a sentence uttered:

HERE WE READ WHAT WE (SHALL) HAVE WRITTEN

COLOPHON

The Isles of Signatories was designed at Coffee House Press, in the historic warehouse district of downtown Minneapolis. Fonts include Avant Garde, Scala Sans, Verdana, and Village.

FUNDER ACKNOWLEDGMENTS

Coffee House Press is an independent nonprofit literary publisher. Our books are made possible through the generous support of grants and gifts from many foundations, corporate giving programs, state and federal support, and through donations from individuals who believe in the transformational power of literature. Coffee House Press receives general operating support from the Minnesota State Arts Board, through an appropriation by the Minnesota State Legislature and from the National Endowment for the Arts, and major general operating support from the McKnight Foundation, and from Target. Coffee House also receives support from: an anonymous donor; the Elmer and Eleanor Andersen Foundation; the Buuck Family Foundation; the Patrick and Aimee Butler Family Foundation; Jennifer Haugh; Stephen and Isabel Keating; Allan and Cinda Kornblum; Mary McDermid; Stu Wilson and Melissa Barker; the Lenfestey Family Foundation; Rebecca Rand; the law firm of Schwegman, Lundberg, Woessner, P.A.; the James R. Thorpe Foundation; the Woessner Freeman Family Foundation; the Wood-Rill Foundation; and many other generous individual donors.

This activity is made possible in part by a grant from the Minnesota State Arts Board, through an appropriation by the Minnesota State Legislature and a grant from the National Endowment for the Arts. MINNESOTA STATE ARTS BOARD

TARGET.

To you and our many readers across the country, we send our thanks for your continuing support.

Good books are brewing
at coffeehousepress.org